JBIOG
Morga
Gallagher, Jim.

Daniel Morgan : fighting
frontiersman /

DANIEL MORGAN

Fighting Frontiersman

FORGOTTEN HEROES
OF THE AMERICAN REVOLUTION

Nathanael Greene: The General Who Saved the Revolution

Henry Knox: Washington's Artilleryman

Francis Marion: Swamp Fox of South Carolina

Daniel Morgan: Fighting Frontiersman

John Stark: Live Free or Die

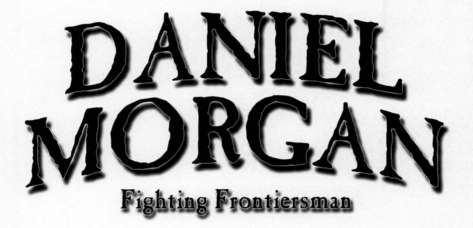

DANIEL MORGAN

Fighting Frontiersman

Jim Gallagher

OTTN PUBLISHING
STOCKTON, NJ

DEDICATION: To my son, Dillon.

Frontispiece: Daniel Morgan and other American officers observe the British surrender at Saratoga. Morgan played a key leadership role during the 1777 Saratoga campaign, and the American victory helped turn the tide of the war in the Patriots' favor.

OTTN Publishing
16 Risler Street
Stockton, NJ 08859
www.ottnpublishing.com

First printing

1 3 5 7 9 8 6 4 2

Library of Congress Cataloging-in-Publication Data

Gallagher, Jim, 1969-
   Daniel Morgan : fighting frontiersman / Jim Gallagher.
      p. cm. — (Forgotten heroes of the American Revolution)
   Includes bibliographical references and index.
   ISBN-13: 978-1-59556-015-5 (hc)
   ISBN-10: 1-59556-015-7 (hc)
   ISBN-13: 978-1-59556-020-9 (pb)
   ISBN-10: 1-59556-020-3 (pb)
   1. Morgan, Daniel, 1736-1802—Juvenile literature. 2. Generals—United
States—Biography—Juvenile literature. 3. United States. Continental
Army—Biography. 4. United States—History—Revolution, 1775-1783—Campaigns—Juvenile literature. 5. Pioneers—Virginia—Winchester—Biography—Juvenile literature. 6. Winchester (Va.)—Biography—Juvenile literature. I. Title.
   E207.M8G35 2006
   973.3'3092—dc22
   [B]

                                        2006020698

Publisher's Note: All quotations in this book come from original sources, and contain the spelling and grammatical inconsistencies of the original text.

TABLE OF CONTENTS

Why Daniel Morgan Should Be Remembered

"Morgan, you have done wonders this day. You have immortalized yourself and honored your country."

—General Horatio Gates, after the battle of Saratoga.

"Sir, you command the finest regiment in the world."

—General John Burgoyne, during the surrender at Saratoga, October 19, 1777.

"The enemy had with their army great numbers of marksmen, armed with rifle-barreled pieces. These, during an engagement, hovered upon the flanks in small detachments, and were very expert in securing themselves, and in shifting their ground. In this action [September 19], many placed themselves in high trees, in the rear of their own line; and there was seldom a minute's interval of smoke in any part of our line, without officers being taken off by single shot."

—Burgoyne, on Morgan's corps, in his report to Parliament on Saratoga.

"Nothing would give me greater pleasure than to have you with me. The people of this country adore you. Had you been with me a few weeks past, you would have had it in your power to give the world the pleasure of reading a second Cowpens affair. . . . Great generals are scarce—there are few Morgans to be found."

—General Nathanael Greene, letter to Daniel Morgan, August 26, 1781.

"I have a great regard for Genl. Morgan, and respect his military talents; am persuaded, if a fit occasion should occur no one would exert them with more zeal in the service of his country than he would."

—George Washington, letter to Colonel Charles M. Thruston, 1794.

"Patriotism and valor were the prominent features of his character; and the honorable services he rendered to his country during the Revolutionary War crowned him with glory and will remain in the breasts of his countrymen a Perpetual Monument to his Memory."

—Epitaph on Daniel Morgan's grave, 1802.

"His courage was of a peculiar quality. . . . When beyond the reach of danger . . . he was accustomed to admit his sensibility to the impressions of fear. Just previous to some of the most glorious occasions of his life, those feelings are said by himself to have come upon him like an apparition, shaking for a moment his inmost soul. But at the crisis of battle most trying to human fortitude, when death presented itself on every side, and danger flew thickly around, no such weakness ever exhibited."

—James Graham, Morgan's first biographer, in
The Life of General Daniel Morgan (1856).

"From Bunker Hill to Quebec, through Burgoyne's campaign, and wherever he was entrusted with command, he had proved his courage and his fertility in resources during periods of great danger; and Congress vied with States and citizens, in honorable testimonials to his valor, as the victor at Cowpens."

—Col. Henry B. Carrington, in *Battles of the American Revolution,*
1775–1781 (1877).

"Morgan, by virtue of his strong personality and commanding presence, could mix freely with his soldiers and acquire their good will without losing their respect. A contemporary wrote that no officer 'knew better how to gain the love and esteem of his men.'"

—Don Higginbotham, in *Daniel Morgan: Revolutionary Rifleman* (1961).

"Brigadier General Daniel Morgan of the Virginia Line was by far the Continental Army's finest battle captain. If one were to judge him by all who have led Americans into battle, he would have no superiors and few peers."

—John Buchanan, in *The Road to Guilford Courthouse:*
The American Revolution in the Carolinas (1997).

SHOWDOWN AT COWPENS

The gently sloping field where Daniel Morgan decided to make a stand against a pursuing British army, known as Cowpens, probably looked something like this on the evening of January 16, 1781. Though General Morgan (opposite) was respected as a battlefield tactician, he faced a stiff challenge at Cowpens.

1

As afternoon faded into evening on January 16, 1781, hundreds of weary men trudged into a grassy, open area near Thicketty Creek, South Carolina. These American soldiers had been on the move all day, trying to elude a pursuing British army. Their commander, Brigadier General Daniel Morgan, had been trying to avoid a battle. Morgan knew that if his outnumbered men were defeated, American hopes for independence might come to an end.

9

The American Revolution was entering its seventh year, and many people were tired of the war. In the northern colonies British and *Patriot* forces were at a *stalemate*, but in the South the British had won a series of victories during 1779 and 1780 and seemed to be regaining control. America's ally France was growing reluctant to waste more soldiers or supplies on what appeared to be a lost cause. The French foreign minister, Comte de Vergennes, had even suggested a peace agreement in which Britain would keep the southern colonies and New York, while Massachusetts, Pennsylvania, and a few other colonies would become independent. Although Patriot leaders did not like this plan, they knew that another major American defeat in the South would force them to accept the French proposal.

CHOOSING THE BATTLEGROUND

By the evening of January 16, Morgan knew his men would have to fight. The British were only a few miles away, and his men were worn out. After carefully scouting the area, he decided his small army of about 1,000 men would offer battle in a grassy pasture that local farmers called Cowpens. Morgan's aide, Captain Dennis Tramell, later recalled that as the general looked out over the terrain, he commented, "Captain, here is Morgan's grave or victory."

Victory would not be easy. The British commander was Lieutenant Colonel Banastre Tarleton, a cunning and ruthless young officer who had become one of the most hated and feared men in the South. Tarleton's force included about 500 members of the British Legion, a crack force of well-trained infantry soldiers and horsemen, along with another 700 British regulars. Also, the terrain at Cowpens did not seem ideal for the Americans. There were no swamps or thick forests that would prevent Tarleton's horsemen from charging into the American lines. The field was so wide that the British infantry might be able to **outflank** the Patriots. Finally, if the fight went badly an American retreat would be blocked by the nearby Broad River, which had been flooded by recent rains. It would be nearly impossible for Morgan's army to escape annihilation by fleeing across the swollen river.

Colonel Banastre Tarleton, wearing the green coat of the British Legion, reaches for his sword in this dashing portrait. Under Tarleton, the Legion had routed Continental soldiers and Patriot militias during several encounters in South Carolina in 1780.

The Americans were anxious to fight, though, and they trusted their commander's judgment. Morgan had won decisive victories in some of the most crucial battles of the Revolution. The tall, solidly built general had a reputation for toughness and bravery, as well as an excellent grasp of battlefield *tactics*. He had developed a special plan for the battle, and he believed his soldiers could carry it out.

First, though, he wanted his tired men to eat and rest. Cowpens was a place where local farmers let their cattle graze before taking them to market, and there was a herd in the open fields. Morgan ordered the soldiers to butcher some of the animals and roast the meat for supper. While darkness fell and the soldiers ate, Morgan explained his battle plan to his officers. After this, the general wandered through the American camp, stopping to visit the small groups of soldiers gathered around flickering campfires.

EXPLAINING THE PLAN

Nearly all of the American soldiers respected Morgan. Unlike most other Continental Army officers, who came from wealthy and privileged backgrounds, Morgan owned a small farm and had once been a wagon driver on the frontier. He had never lost his connection to the regular soldiers, sharing their hardships in the field and worrying about their problems and fears. On the night of January 16, Morgan carefully explained to his men what they would have to do to defeat the British the next morning.

Morgan spent most of his time speaking to the *militia* that accompanied his force. All Continental officers knew that these untrained, inexperienced volunteer soldiers often ran away when facing a British bayonet charge. However, the militia had an essential role to play in Morgan's battle plan. The men responded eagerly to the commander's confidence. "It was upon this occasion that I was more perfectly convinced of General Morgan's qualifications to command militia, than I had ever before been," commented Thomas Young, a militia major from South Carolina.

> The evening previous to the battle, he went among the volunteers, helped them fix their swords, joked with them about their sweet-hearts, told them to keep in good spirits, and the day would be ours. And long after I laid down, he was going about among the soldiers, encouraging them, and telling them that the "Old Wagoner" would crack his whip over Ben [Tarleton] in the morning, as sure as he lived. "Just hold up your heads, boys," he would say, "three fires, and you are free! And then when you return to your homes, how the old folks will bless you, and the girls kiss you, for your gallant conduct!" I don't believe he slept a wink that night.

Morgan was not the only person keeping late hours. Tarleton knew the Americans were near, so he drove his exhausted men through the night to reach them. At dawn on the chilly morning of January 17, 1781, the British marched up the road to Cowpens. They found Morgan's men in the field and ready to fight. Shouting their battle cry, the British soldiers lowered their bayonets and charged through the damp grass toward the American lines.

LIFE ON THE FRONTIER

Very little is known for certain about Daniel Morgan's early life. As an adult, Morgan did not like to talk about his childhood. This may mean his family life was not very happy or pleasant. His parents were Welsh immigrants who arrived in America during the 1720s. Daniel was probably born on the family farm in rural Hunterdon County, New Jersey, in 1735 or 1736; the exact date is unknown.

When Daniel Morgan was about 17 years old he had a bitter argument with his father, and during the winter of 1752–53 he decided to leave home. Morgan traveled west across Pennsylvania, then south through Maryland and into Virginia. His journey ended after he crossed the Blue Ridge

Mountains and reached the frontier village of Winchester, Virginia. Established in 1744, Winchester contained about 60 homes, stores, taverns, and churches when Morgan arrived in the spring of 1753. In the countryside around Winchester, families cleared land, built log cabins, and established small farms.

Morgan first took a job with a farmer named Roberts. He was a hard worker, so Roberts made him foreman of his sawmill. But a wealthy landowner named Robert Burwell soon offered Morgan more money to work as a *teamster*, or wagon driver. Morgan took the job. He enjoyed the freedom of driving a wagon over the lonely country roads. In a year he saved enough to buy his own wagon and horses.

Morgan soon left Burwell to work as an independent freight hauler. He found steady work transporting flour, salt, and other supplies from Winchester to Fort Cumberland, a British outpost on the Maryland frontier. The fort, which had been built to prevent Indian attacks, usually held just a few soldiers. But in the spring of 1755, a large British army had arrived at Fort Cumberland. The British commander, General Edward Braddock, had been sent to drive a French army out of the nearby Ohio River valley.

WAR COMES TO THE OHIO VALLEY

For years, Britain and France had been enemies, fighting for power in Europe and elsewhere. Each had established colonies in the New World. The French controlled Montreal, Quebec, and other settlements in Canada. France also claimed much of North America, including the Great Lakes and the territory drained by the Mississippi River as far south as Louisiana. By contrast, Britain's 13 North American colonies existed on a narrow strip of land along the Atlantic coast. In the 1750s, practically all of the British settlements were within 200 miles of the ocean. However, the British colonies were growing quickly, and newcomers seeking land continually pushed the frontier west.

—FAST FACT—

The French territories in North America were sparsely populated. Most French colonists were trappers and fur traders who lived solitary, nomadic lives in the wilderness.

This westward expansion annoyed French leaders, who wanted to control the territory beyond the Appalachian Mountains. It also angered Native Americans, who were forced from their lands as the British colonies grew. The Indians and French agreed to work together to force the British out of North America.

During the early 1750s, French soldiers began building forts in the Ohio River valley. One outpost, Fort Duquesne, occupied a strategic spot on the Ohio River. The British wanted to control the river because it could be used to move people and goods west from the colonies. When the French refused British demands to leave, Braddock was sent with 2,400 British soldiers to force them out.

BRADDOCK'S EXPEDITION

By June 1755, Braddock's expedition was nearly ready, but he needed wagons to carry supplies. To solve this problem, Braddock ordered Morgan and other wagon drivers to accompany him. The teamsters were not happy about being forced to join Braddock's expedition. Like Morgan, they were frontiersmen who enjoyed their freedom. The civilian wagon drivers were also not prepared for the British army's strict rules. Wagon drivers were often whipped for drinking, fighting, or breaking camp rules.

One time, Morgan was whipped for punching a British officer who had insulted him. Morgan's punishment was 500 lashes, and before the flogging ended his back was bloody and raw. Although he carried the scars for the rest of his life, years later Morgan was able to joke about the incident. He claimed that he had heard the drummer miscount the lashes, so that he received only 499. "I did not think it worthwhile to tell him of his mistake, and let it go," he told a friend.

As the expedition moved slowly north, Braddock divided his army. The general pressed ahead with about 1,300 soldiers while the rest guarded the slow-moving supply wagons. On July 9, 1755, Braddock's advance force was approaching Fort Duquesne when the air was suddenly filled with the whizzing of musket balls and the sound of war whoops. The British had stumbled into an ambush. French soldiers and their Indian allies shot the redcoats down from behind rocks and trees. Braddock tried to rally the troops, but he was mortally wounded. His aide, a 22-year-old Virginia militia colonel named George Washington, supervised the British retreat.

When the survivors of the battle reached the supply wagons, Morgan and other teamsters helped destroy ammunition and supplies to make room on their wagons for wounded soldiers. The remnants of Braddock's army soon returned to Fort Cumberland, and Morgan returned home to Winchester.

Wounded British general Edward Braddock is carried on an ammunition wagon as the remnants of his army retreat from Fort Duquesne, July 1755.

GAINING MILITARY EXPERIENCE

With the British army beaten, Native Americans began to launch daring raids against frontier settlements. In Virginia, the colonial government ordered the militia to defend the frontier. Morgan joined a company of rangers, soldiers who would use their skills as woodsmen to find and fight the enemy. In September 1755, the rangers headed to the south branch of the Potomac River, where Morgan and the other men built small **stockades**. These crude forts were about 90 feet square, with high walls made of logs that had been sharpened to points at the top. While patrolling the frontier, the men lived in simple log huts inside the stockade walls.

In addition to scouting for the enemy, Morgan helped guide militia companies and supply wagons between British outposts. This could be very dangerous. On one trip in April 1756, seven Indians ambushed Morgan and another ranger. Morgan's friend was killed, and a musket ball hit Morgan in the mouth, breaking several teeth and tearing through his cheek. Despite the shock and pain, Morgan was able to quickly turn his horse and escape. By the time he arrived at Fort Edwards, 14 miles away, he was delirious from pain. Although the wound left a permanent scar, Morgan soon recovered and returned to duty. He served with the rangers until October 1756, when the unit was disbanded because the Indian threat had diminished.

FUN-LOVING BRAWLER

Historians are not sure how Morgan spent the next two years. Some believe he joined another militia unit serving near Winchester. Others say he withdrew to a cabin in the wilderness, avoiding other people and hunting wild game for food. But by November 1758, when a British force captured Fort Duquesne, Morgan had definitely resumed his career as a wagon driver. For the next few years, he carried crops like wheat, flax, and tobacco from Winchester to larger settlements such as Alexandria, Dumfries, Fredericksburg, and Falmouth. On his return trips, he brought goods that were needed on the frontier, such as grindstones, tar, nails, sugar, and salt. Morgan got to know the countryside very well. He would later write that he was "as well acquainted with the roads as any man in Virginia."

From his letters, as well as from court records, historians know that Morgan spent his spare time with a wild group of friends. They hunted, raced horses, gambled, drank rum, and occasionally got into fistfights. Morgan was fun to be around. He liked to tell jokes and stories about his military experiences. He was larger than most of his friends, at just over six feet tall with broad shoulders and thick muscles. Morgan was very strong and also very competitive. He was always ready to fight or race anyone who challenged him, and he rarely lost. He was a proud man and had a terrible temper when he felt insulted. However, he was always loyal to his friends, even when they got into trouble with the law.

SETTLING DOWN

Eventually, Morgan settled down. In 1761 the 25-year-old began courting Abigail Curry, the teenaged daughter of a local farmer. By 1763 they were living together on a rented farm. By the time they married in 1773, Abigail had given birth to two daughters, Nancy and Betsy.

Morgan went back to war briefly during 1763. That year, the French and Indian War had officially ended. Britain had gained control of French lands in North America, and this made many Native Americans unhappy. In May an Ottawa war leader named Pontiac inspired Indians to attack British forts on the frontier. Once again Virginia called out the militia, and Morgan was appointed a lieutenant in one company. Morgan's troops did not see any action during Chief Pontiac's War, though, and after a few months he and his men were able to return home.

Over the next few years, Morgan became more interested in farming. By 1769 he had sold his wagon, and in 1771 Morgan bought a 255-acre farm near Winchester. The purchase took most of his money, but he soon made the farm profitable. During this time, Morgan taught himself how to read. He also began to take a greater interest in public

By the KING,

A PROCLAMATION,

Declaring the Ceffation of Arms, as well by Sea as Land, agreed upon between His Majefty, the Moft Chriftian King, and the Catholick King, and enjoining the Obfervance thereof.

GEORGE R.

HEREAS Preliminaries for reftoring Peace were figned at *Fontainebleau*, on the Third Day of this Inftant *November*, by the Minifters of Us, the Moft Chriftian King, and the Catholic King: And whereas for the putting an End to the Calamities of War, as foon and as far as may be poffible, it has been agreed between Us, His Moft Chriftian Majefty, and His Catholick Majefty, as follows ; that is to fay,

That as foon as the Preliminaries fhall be figned and ratified, all Hoftilities fhould ceafe at Sea and at Land.

And to prevent all Occafions of Complaints and Difputes which might arife upon account of Ships, Merchandizes, and other Effects, which might be taken at Sea ; it has been alfo mutually agreed, That the Ships, Merchandizes, and Effects, which fhould be taken in the *Channel*, and in the *North Seas*, after the Space of Twelve Days, to be computed from the Ratification of the prefent Preliminary Articles ; and that all Ships, Merchandizes, and Effects, which fhould be taken after Six Weeks from the faid Ratification, beyond the *Channel*, the *Britifh Seas*, and the *North Seas*, as far as the *Canary Iflands* inclufively, whether in the Ocean, or *Mediterranean* ; and for the Space of Three Months, from the faid *Canary Iflands* to the *Equinoctial Line* or *Equator* ; and for the Space of Six Months, beyond the faid *Equinoctial Line* or *Equator*, and in all other Places of the World, without any Exception, or other more particular Diftinction of Time or Place, fhould be reftored on both Sides.

And whereas the Ratifications of the faid Preliminary Articles, in due Form, were exchanged at *Verfailles*, by the Plenipotentiaries of Us, of the Moft Chriftian King, and of the Catholick King, on the Twenty fecond of this Inftant *November*, from which Day the feveral Terms above-mentioned of Twelve Days, of Six Weeks, of Three Months, and of Six Months, for the Reftitution of all Ships, Merchandizes, and other Effects, taken at Sea, are to be computed.

We have thought fit, by and with the Advice of Our Privy Council, to notify the fame to all Our loving Subjects: and We do declare, That Our Royal Will and Pleafure is, and We do hereby ftrictly Charge and Command all Our Officers, both at Sea and Land, and all other Our Subjects whatfoever, to forbear all Acts of Hoftility, either by Sea or Land, againft His Moft Chriftian Majefty, and His Catholick Majefty, Their Vaffals, or Subjects, from and after the refpective Times above-mentioned, and under the Penalty of incurring Our higheft Difpleafure.

Given at Our Court at *Saint James's*, the Twenty fixth Day of *November*, in the Third Year of Our Reign, and in the Year of Our Lord 1762.

God fave the King.

A proclamation issued by Britain's King George III announcing the end of the French and Indian War. In the aftermath of the conflict, the British government began imposing new taxes and other restrictive policies on the colonies. These stirred up resentment among the Americans, some of whom began to talk of independence.

affairs. As he became a respected member of the Winchester community, Morgan was appointed a road supervisor. This part-time job involved making sure important roads in the county were maintained. He was also promoted to captain in the militia.

—FAST FACT—

Like many landowners in colonial America, Daniel Morgan used African slaves to work his farm. By 1774 he owned 10 slaves. Although this meant that Morgan was quite prosperous by frontier standards, for a wealthy Virginia planter 10 would be a paltry number of slaves. George Washington, for example, owned about 135 slaves.

In 1774 Morgan went to war again. To keep peace with the Indians along the frontier, in 1763 Britain's King George III had declared that Americans could not move west of the Appalachian Mountains. This angered many settlers, who chose to disobey the king. The expansion of British settlements drove the Shawnee and Mingo tribes to attack settlers in western Virginia in June 1774. In response the colony's governor, Lord Dunmore, sent the militia to defend the colonists. The Virginia militia fought several *skirmishes* and destroyed a number of villages. In the fall of 1774, the Indians agreed to peace. Morgan, who commanded about 50 soldiers, later described his part in Lord Dunmore's War as "very active and hard."

Although Lord Dunmore's War ended quickly, another clash was on the horizon. This one, however, would not be resolved so easily. It would pit the American colonists against the government that ruled them from Great Britain.

3

MORGAN THE RIFLEMAN

King George's Proclamation of 1763 was not the only royal order that had annoyed the colonists. During the 1760s the British government imposed many new taxes that Americans considered unfair. Protests and riots occurred throughout the 1760s and early 1770s. Most people hoped the situation could be resolved peacefully. But after April 1775, when British soldiers and American militiamen fought at Lexington and Concord, war seemed unavoidable.

In Philadelphia, representatives of each of the 13 colonies except Georgia gathered in May to discuss the crisis. The Continental Congress, as this colonial assembly became known, decided to write to King George and ask him to

WEAPONS OF THE 18TH-CENTURY SOLDIER

During the American Revolution, most soldiers fought with muskets and bayonets. Muskets were only accurate at close range, so soldiers had to move quite close to their enemy during battle. When fighting in an open field, the soldiers would form lines and advance. The first line would fire a volley, as shown in the illustration at right, then drop to a knee to reload as the men standing in the next line fired their muskets. By the time the smoke cleared, the men in the first line were ready to fire another volley. This concentrated fire was meant to disrupt the enemy's lines. If an enemy unit panicked and moved out of position, the attacking infantrymen could attach their bayonets—deadly knives, usually 15 to 20 inches long—to the ends of the muskets and charge the retreating enemy.

This style of fighting required great discipline. If soldiers became confused or ran away from an enemy charge, it could cause a break in the battle line that would imperil the entire army. Infantry soldiers needed intensive training so they could maneuver effectively in battle and stand up to bayonet charges.

An American musket (top), along with a socket bayonet that could be fitted into the barrel to make a deadly close-range weapon. (bottom) Most British soldiers were equipped with the Short Land Service Pattern musket, commonly called the "Brown Bess."

An American musket cartridge (right), wrapped in a piece of an old letter. Soldiers usually carried 17 to 24 musket rounds into battle in cases like the one shown.

Detail of the firing mechanism of a British musket.

A bayonet (above) found on the battlefield at Guilford Courthouse.

change his policies. In its message, known as the Olive Branch Petition, Congress promised that the colonies would remain loyal if the king treated them fairly.

At the same time, however, Congress recognized that the king would probably not agree to the American requests. Britain had one of the strongest armies in the world. The king could send troops and force the colonists to obey his commands—unless the Americans had an army of their own. On June 14, 1775, Congress voted to create an army of 20,000 men. The experienced Virginian George Washington was placed in command of this new force, called the Continental Army.

SHARPSHOOTER COMMANDER

Like the British troops, most of the Continental soldiers would be armed with muskets and bayonets. But Congress decided that the army should also include 10 companies of frontiersmen from western Pennsylvania, Maryland, and Virginia. These men would be armed with long rifles, which were more accurate than muskets. With muskets, it was hard to hit a man-sized target at more than 50 yards. With a long rifle, an experienced frontiersman could easily hit a seven-inch target 200 yards away. The rifle units would be used to support regular infantry units. They would serve as sharpshooters, go on scouting patrols, or harass the enemy using guerrilla tactics.

WEAPONS OF THE 18TH-CENTURY RIFLEMAN

Daniel Morgan's men were armed with long rifles, unique weapons developed on the frontier that were accurate at 200 yards or more. Spiral grooves cut inside the rifle's four-foot-long barrel caused the projectile—a lead ball wrapped in cloth—to spin rapidly when fired. This made the ball fly farther and straighter than a musket ball.

The rifle's accuracy and range were great advantages, but the weapons had some disadvantages in battle as well. A rifle took longer to load than a musket. Also, bayonets could not be mounted on rifles because they would damage the barrels, so riflemen often had to run away from British bayonet charges.

Long rifles like this one were made by artisans on the American frontier, and riflemen serving with Morgan's company carried their personal weapons.

Because all long rifles were different, riflemen made their own bullets for their weapons by pouring hot lead into bullet molds like the one below.

Riflemen carried powder horns like the one above to keep their gunpowder dry.

For hand-to-hand fighting, riflemen carried tomahawks or long knives (above).

Because of Morgan's war experience and reputation, he was placed in charge of one of Virginia's two rifle companies. He immediately began enlisting the best marksmen he could find. On July 15, Morgan started his 96 men on the 600-mile march to Boston.

When the riflemen arrived three weeks later, they found that the Americans held strong forts in the hills around Boston. The British would not come out of the city to attack them. Morgan's riflemen impressed the Continental soldiers by shooting British officers who were out of musket range. However, the riflemen wanted action, and they soon grew bored with camp life.

THE LONG TREK TO CANADA

Morgan was pleased when his company was chosen to take part in an American invasion of Canada. A bold young colonel named Benedict Arnold had developed the plan. Arnold had already distinguished himself in the war. In May 1775, commanding fewer than 100 men, he had captured Fort Ticonderoga and other important British outposts on Lake Champlain. These victories provided the American army with more than 200 cannons, as well as gunpowder and other essential military supplies. After this success, Arnold convinced Congress that with an army, he could capture Quebec and other British cities in Canada. Congress was interested because gaining control of Quebec would make it difficult for British reinforcements to land in North America. However, seizing the city would not be easy. Quebec was the strongest fortress in North America. It was located on a steep hill above the St. Lawrence River and surrounded by thick stone walls.

The Americans planned a two-pronged invasion. General Richard Montgomery, an American who had once served in the British army, would lead about 3,000 soldiers north from Lake Champlain and capture Montreal. From there, Montgomery's army would follow the St. Lawrence River northeast to Quebec. At the same time, Colonel Arnold would lead 800 infantrymen and 300 riflemen through the Maine wilderness. The two armies would unite at Quebec to attack the British stronghold.

On September 11, 1775, Arnold's men boarded ships and sailed to Gardiner, Maine. When they arrived, Arnold and Morgan, who had been placed in charge of all the riflemen, led their men north. The journey was exhausting and

American soldiers carry their boats and supplies between rivers on the march to Quebec. The journey through the wilderness was exhausting. A rifleman named Joseph Henry wrote in his journal that Morgan's men had the flesh "worn from their shoulders, even to the bone."

dangerous. The soldiers had planned to use small boats to move their supplies north through the wilderness. However, they were fighting a swift current, and the men often had to *portage* around rapids and waterfalls. This slowed their progress. Morgan's frontiersmen scouted the terrain ahead of the main army. Morgan worked along with his men, cutting down trees and bushes as they tried to clear a road.

As the army struggled north, enduring rain and snow, the soldiers' clothes grew ragged and their shoes wore out. Things were so bad that 300 soldiers from New England abandoned the mission and went home. Every day, men were dying of disease. The greatest danger, though, was starvation. By late October the men were nearly out of food. Arnold sent out parties to *forage* for supplies to keep his army alive. On November 9, Arnold's remaining soldiers arrived at Point Levis, across the St. Lawrence River from Quebec. Only about 600 Americans had completed the grueling 350-mile journey.

PLAN OF ATTACK

Arnold wanted to attack immediately, but a bad storm made crossing the river impossible for several days. On the night of November 13, Arnold sneaked his men across the river and led them along a steep, narrow path up the cliff. The next morning, British guards awoke to find the Americans camped in front of the city.

General Richard Montgomery was an experienced soldier, having served with the British army during the French and Indian War. After purchasing a farm in New York, Montgomery supported the Patriots in their struggle for independence. Because of his military experience, Montgomery was placed in charge of the invasion of Canada.

The British troops knew they were safe inside Quebec's strong walls, so they did not come out to fight. On November 19, the Americans withdrew to Point Aux Trembles, about 25 miles away, to meet Montgomery's army. Morgan was placed in charge of the rear guard, which meant his men would have to defend the army if the British attacked during the march.

General Montgomery arrived at Point Aux Trembles on December 1. Although his army had captured Montreal, like Arnold's it had been dramatically reduced by disease and desertion. The combined American army totaled about 975 men. In the meantime, Quebec had been reinforced and was now defended by about 1,800 men. The British also had more than 200 cannons, while the Americans had just 6—and they were too small to damage the city's walls. Winter had arrived in Canada, and the Americans were suffering from exposure to the cold and shortages of food. The British, however, had warm homes and plenty of food stored to withstand a *siege*.

Montgomery and Arnold decided to attack early on the morning of December 31. Quebec consisted of a walled upper town, where the British troops stayed, and a lower town along the river, where there were shops and homes. A gate in the center of the lower town connected it to the upper town. The American plan was for a small force to create a diversion outside the walls of the upper town. At the same time, Arnold would attack the lower town from the north and Montgomery would lead an assault from the south. If all went as planned, the Americans would meet at the gate, surprise the British defenders, and rush into the upper town.

THE ASSAULT ON QUEBEC

Snow was falling as Morgan and his riflemen entered the lower town. Suddenly, alarm bells began to ring—the Americans had been spotted. Morgan and his men ran through the narrow streets toward the gate. At one street, they found British soldiers defending a wooden barrier. Arnold shouted to the men to charge the barrier. Suddenly, the colonel fell into the snow, hit in the leg with a musket ball.

Arnold was carried from the battlefield, and the other officers asked Morgan to lead the charge against the British barrier. He placed a ladder against its side and was the first over the top. A blast from the defenders' muskets nearly killed him—one ball tore through his hat, while another grazed his cheek. Startled, Morgan fell backwards into the snow, and his worried men crowded around him. But the captain quickly regained his feet and climbed the ladder again. This time, he leapt over the top of the barrier. More Americans followed, and the British soldiers surrendered.

Morgan could see that the gate to the upper town was undefended. The British seemed to be on the run, and he

Morgan and the Americans are trapped by British soldiers near the gate to Quebec's upper town. "[We] took everything that opposed us at the point of the bayonet till we arrived at the barrier gate," Morgan later wrote. "Here I was ordered to wait for Gen. Montgomery, and a fatal order it was. It prevented me from taking the garrison, as I had already made half the town prisoners."

wanted to press ahead. But he could not convince the other officers, who wanted to wait for Montgomery. Morgan was angry and upset, but he had no choice.

What Morgan and the other officers did not know was that Montgomery and his men would never arrive. As they had approached the city, a British cannon blast killed the general and several of his men. The rest of Montgomery's force had retreated.

If the Americans inside Quebec had followed Morgan, they might have won an amazing victory. The assault had confused and disheartened the British, and their commander briefly considered surrendering. But when the Americans failed to press into the upper town, the redcoats rallied. When Morgan's men finally tried to advance several hours later, the British were ready. A fierce battle raged in the streets around the gate. Morgan encouraged his men to charge the enemy as cannons boomed and muskets crashed. George Morison, an American soldier who took part in the battle, later wrote, "Betwixt every peal the awful voice of Morgan is heard, whose gigantic stature and terrible appearance carries dismay among the foe wherever he comes."

SURRENDER AND IMPRISONMENT

Despite Morgan's efforts, the battle was hopeless. British soldiers were firing from inside houses, and the Americans soon found themselves surrounded. As his men began to throw down their weapons, Morgan angrily refused to surrender. He drew his sword and dared the British soldiers to come and get him. They threatened to shoot Morgan, while the American riflemen begged their leader to give up and save his life. Then Morgan saw a French priest in the crowd of citizens who had gathered to watch this strange scene. He handed the priest his sword, saying, "Not a scoundrel of those cowards shall take it out of my hands."

The invasion of Canada was a disaster for the Patriots. Four hundred Americans were captured during the battle for Quebec, and another 100 were killed, while the British lost just 20 men. Morgan and his men were imprisoned in the city. The British officers admired Morgan's courage and treated him well. He was even invited to become an officer in the British army, but he refused.

Morgan remained a prisoner until September 1776, when he was allowed to go home on *parole*. This was a common practice, in which captured soldiers were released if they promised not to resume fighting until they were exchanged for prisoners captured by the enemy. Morgan would not be allowed to fight again until the American and British armies officially exchanged their prisoners in January 1777.

4

VICTORY AT SARATOGA

When Morgan returned home, he was pleased to learn that his leadership and bravery during the invasion of Canada had impressed George Washington. The American commander in chief had asked Congress to promote Morgan to colonel and to give him command of a new regiment of troops from Virginia. As soon as Morgan was officially exchanged, he headed for the Continental Army's camp in Morristown, New Jersey.

In the spring of 1777, the situation looked bleak for the Patriots. Washington commanded just 9,000 Continentals, while the British army commanded by General William Howe numbered 27,000 men. A second British army of about 8,000 soldiers, under General John Burgoyne, was

General George Washington, pictured here after the Battle of Princeton in January 1777, intended to use Morgan's riflemen to disrupt British campaigns.

preparing to march south from Quebec. If they worked together, Howe and Burgoyne could crush the Continental Army between them.

Washington knew that such a defeat would probably end the Revolution, so he wanted to avoid a major battle. He had told Congress that for the Patriots to succeed, they needed an army that could "look the enemy in the face." As long as the Continental Army was in the field, the British would have to react to its movements. Instead of attacking the British directly, Washington's soldiers would harass and frustrate the redcoats. Whenever the British made a tactical mistake, the Continentals would attack, but they would always try to leave themselves a way to escape.

"GALL THEM AS MUCH AS POSSIBLE"

Morgan's riflemen were ideal for this type of hit-and-run fighting, so in June 1777, when Howe's army moved into New Jersey, Washington ordered Morgan to follow. "[Y]ou are to . . . watch, with very small Scouting Parties . . . the Enemy's left Flank, and particularly the Roads leading from Brunswick towards Millstone, Princeton, [etc.]," Washington wrote to Morgan on June 13. "In case of any Movement of the Enemy, you are Instantly to fall upon their Flank, and gall them as much as possible, taking especial care not to be surrounded, or have your retreat to the Army cut off."

The next day Morgan's scouts reported that Howe's army was moving in their direction. Morgan's men hid in a wooded area. When the British arrived, the Americans opened fire, forcing them to retreat. When British troops pressed forward again, Morgan used a whistle to signal his men to fall back. The Americans withdrew to a hill that would

A camouflaged member of Morgan's rifle unit goes on patrol. The riflemen excelled at harassing British troops on the march.

be easy to defend. The British, frustrated, returned to New Brunswick.

On June 21, Howe ordered a retreat to Amboy, near New York, hoping to draw Washington into a battle. This time Morgan and his men were sent as part of a larger force commanded by General Nathanael Greene. At the urging of Morgan and another aggressive officer, General Anthony Wayne, the Americans attacked the British rear guard. In a report to Congress on the attack, Washington wrote, "In the pursuit, Colo Morgan's Rifle Men exchanged several sharp Fires with the Enemy. . . . Genl Greene desires me to make mention of the Conduct and bravery of Genl. Wayne and Colo. Morgan and of their Officers and Men upon this occasion, as they constantly advanced upon an Enemy far superior to them in numbers and well secured behind strong *Redoubts*."

HALTING BURGOYNE'S ADVANCE

Howe soon moved his army across the Hudson River to New York. Morgan was ordered to patrol the river and watch the British movements. Washington feared that Howe's army would sail up the Hudson River and join General Burgoyne's army, which had already captured Fort Ticonderoga and was trying to reach Albany. If the British succeeded, they would control the Hudson River and cut off New England from the rest of the colonies. But Howe had a different plan. On July 24, he loaded his men onto ships and set out to sea.

Washington worried about Howe's intentions, but he also understood that Burgoyne had to be stopped. In late July he sent Benedict Arnold, who had been promoted to general and was one of his most trusted officers, to help the Continental Army in western New York. On August 17, Washington sent Morgan and his riflemen to New York. "I know of no Corps so likely to check [Burgoyne's] progress in proportion to their number, as the one you Command," Washington wrote to Morgan. "I have great dependence on you, your Officers and Men."

The riflemen arrived at the American camp on August 30. That evening Morgan ate dinner with General Horatio Gates, the Continental commander. Gates, who had been appointed to the post only a month earlier, did not look much like a soldier. He was short, wore glasses, and had thin gray hair. However, he had spent more than 25 years as an officer in the British army before settling in America. Since taking command in New York, Gates had been working with Arnold to prepare the American army of about 6,200 men to face Burgoyne.

The campaign had been a difficult one for the redcoats. Although their advance into New York had not been stopped, American militiamen had been picking away at the army for months. By late summer, Burgoyne's force had shrunk to

A courageous and experienced British soldier, General John Burgoyne was also proud and overconfident. Burgoyne had promised King George III that he could capture New York and cut off New England from the rest of the colonies.

5,500 men. A second British army of about 2,000 men under General Barry St. Leger, which was traveling east along the Mohawk River, was turned back by the Americans in August before it could reinforce Burgoyne. The British troops were also having a hard time finding food and supplies because they had traveled so far from their base in Canada.

On September 8, Gates marched his American army north to a rocky hillside called Bemis Heights, where they built strong fortifications. Morgan's riflemen were sent to watch Burgoyne and harass his scouts. The riflemen were so effective that by September 18, British scouts dared not venture beyond their lines. This meant Burgoyne could not get critical information about the Americans, such as how strong their defenses were.

THE BATTLE OF FREEMAN'S FARM

Though hampered by the lack of information, Burgoyne decided to approach Bemis Heights on September 19. He divided his army into three columns. On the left were 1,200 Hessian *mercenaries* commanded by Major General Baron von Riedesel. Burgoyne commanded 1,100 British soldiers in the center column. On the right, Brigadier General Simon Fraser was in charge of 2,200 British soldiers, *Loyalists*, and Indians allied with the British.

When Gates learned the British were approaching, he sent Morgan's corps to attack them in the woods. Morgan's men advanced so quickly that they ran into Burgoyne's center column. The surprised riflemen initially retreated, but Morgan used his whistle to call his men back together. While Morgan's men regrouped, the British soldiers prepared for battle on a nearby farm owned by a Loyalist named Isaac Freeman.

At around 1 P.M. Morgan's men charged the enemy. They captured some British cannons, but the British drove them back with a bayonet charge and recaptured the guns. The riflemen retreated to the nearby woods. From hiding places among the trees, they began to shoot British artillerymen and officers. The riflemen were outnumbered and in danger of being overwhelmed until General Arnold realized what was happening and sent more American soldiers to help.

The two armies were evenly matched, and they battled back and forth all afternoon. By 5 P.M., Morgan's riflemen had killed most of Burgoyne's artillerymen and officers. But when General Riedesel's mercenaries entered the battle, the Americans decided to withdraw. Night was falling and they were low on ammunition, so Arnold and Morgan led their men back to Bemis Heights.

Although technically a British victory, the Battle of Freeman's Farm cost Burgoyne dearly. About 600 British soldiers had been killed or wounded, compared with 320 American casualties. Morgan's corps had nearly wiped out an entire British infantry regiment, killing or wounding more than 180 men. The riflemen had also shot so many artillerymen that the British could not use their cannons. After the battle, a British captain named Thomas Anburey wrote in his journal that he was "astonished" at how fiercely the Americans had fought. "They are not that contemptible enemy we had

Horatio Gates was an experienced officer who had served in the British army for 25 years before retiring to Virginia. When the Revolution began, he took up the Patriot cause and helped organize the Continental Army. However, he had practically no experience in battle—the only combat he had seen before the Saratoga campaign was as a member of Braddock's ill-fated expedition in 1755.

hitherto thought them, incapable of standing a regular engagement, and that they would only fight behind strong and powerful works," he noted.

THE BATTLE OF BEMIS HEIGHTS

Both armies were exhausted, but Burgoyne soon received good news. The British general Henry Clinton, who was occupying New York City with 4,000 redcoats, had offered to make a *foray* up the Hudson River to help. But it would take weeks for Clinton to arrive. In the meantime, the Americans skirmished regularly with Burgoyne's scouts and camp guards. "Not a single night passes but there is firing and continual attacks," wrote Anburey. The Americans also caught and destroyed British supply wagons coming from Canada, so Burgoyne's men were slowly starving.

Although Gates's strategy seemed to be working, tensions were high among the officers in the American camp. After the Battle of Freeman's Farm, Gates sent Congress a report that did not mention the important role Benedict Arnold had played in the engagement. Arnold, a proud and ambitious man, was offended. When he angrily insulted Gates, Arnold was removed from command.

Morgan had not been mentioned in the report either, but unlike Arnold he ignored the slight and went about his duties. Another incident showed that Gates clearly recognized the importance of Morgan and his men. After

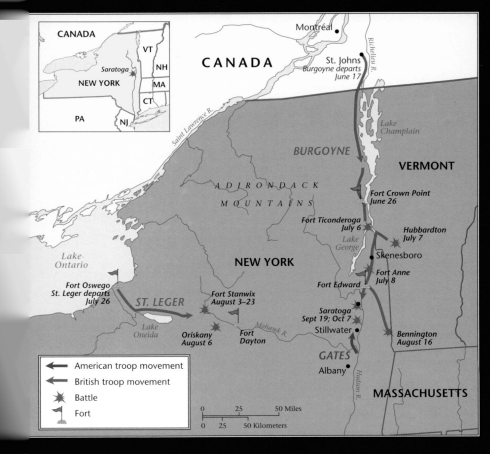

General John Burgoyne's 1777 invasion from Canada (above) was stopped after major engagements at Freeman's Farm and Bemis Heights (below).

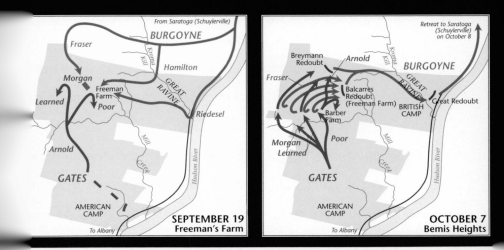

learning about the American success at Freeman's Farm, George Washington had written to Gates asking him to send Morgan's riflemen back to his army. Howe's British force had landed in Maryland, and Washington was trying to prevent Howe from marching north and capturing Philadelphia, the American capital. Gates told Washington that he could not spare the riflemen. "In this situation, your Excellency would not wish me to part with the corps the army of General Burgoyne are most afraid of," Gates wrote on October 5.

On October 7, Burgoyne marched with 2,000 men to a wheat field near Bemis Heights. Gates was unsure of what to do, so Morgan came up with a plan. His men would sneak through the woods and attack the right side of the British lines. At the same time, another American force would attack the British left. Pleased with the plan, Gates told Morgan to "begin the game."

Morgan's men had already scouted the territory, and they knew how to use the terrain to their advantage. They surprised the British, who were forced to retreat. The British left was also driven back, so the Americans then turned to attack the center of Burgoyne's lines.

The outcome hung in the balance until General Arnold arrived on the battlefield. Arnold, who had left camp without Gates's permission, took command of a Continental *brigade*. Shouting encouragement to the soldiers, he directed them to surround the enemy. The battle soon turned into a rout, and Burgoyne could not stop his men from running away.

For a few moments it appeared that another British general, Simon Fraser, might rally the men. When Morgan saw this, he ordered his riflemen to shoot the brave general. Fraser soon fell, mortally wounded, and the British lines collapsed completely. The redcoats ran for their fortified camp at Freeman's Farm.

The Americans had won the field, but they were not ready to stop fighting. Morgan and Arnold, sensing an opportunity to destroy Burgoyne's army completely, led their men after

As night falls on October 7, 1777, Americans led by Arnold and Morgan pursue Hessian soldiers running for their lives toward the British camp at Freeman's Farm.

the fleeing British. With Arnold shouting "Victory or death," the Americans stormed a temporary fortification on a hill near the British camp. After brutal hand-to-hand fighting, the Americans captured it as night fell. From this redoubt, the Americans could fire captured cannons down into the British camp. Burgoyne had no choice but to retreat, leaving behind essential supplies and wounded men.

BURGOYNE'S SURRENDER

The Continental Army had won a brilliant victory. Burgoyne had again lost more than 600 men, while the Americans had suffered just 150 casualties. Over the next few days, Burgoyne moved north along the Hudson River. He still hoped that Clinton's reinforcements would arrive, but the Continentals gradually surrounded the sick and starving British soldiers. On October 17, with Clinton's army still 100 miles away, Burgoyne surrendered his army at the village of Saratoga.

The news that an entire British army had been captured shocked the world and inspired the Patriots. Most important, the victory at Saratoga helped bring France into the war on the American side. French leaders saw the American Revolution as a way to weaken their longtime rival, Britain, but did not want to get involved until the Patriots proved they could win. In early 1778, France made an alliance with the colonies and began sending money and military supplies to America.

Although historians have argued over whether Horatio Gates or Benedict Arnold deserves credit for the American success, there is no question that Daniel Morgan played a critical role. His riflemen were involved in the heaviest fighting at both of the major battles, and they had hindered and harassed the British throughout the campaign. After the Battle of Bemis Heights, Gates reportedly hugged the tough colonel, saying, "Morgan, you have done wonders." In his report to Congress on the battle, Gates wrote, "Too much praise cannot be given to the Corps commanded by Col. Morgan."

General Burgoyne hands his sword to Horatio Gates (center) at Saratoga. Daniel Morgan, wearing the buckskins of a frontiersman, is pictured standing to Gates's left. According to James Graham's 1856 account of Morgan's life, when Burgoyne met Morgan the defeated British general shook his hand and said, "Sir, you command the finest regiment in the world."

5

SUCCESS AND FRUSTRATION

After the victory at Saratoga, Morgan's corps rejoined Washington's army in Pennsylvania. General Howe had captured Philadelphia, so the Continental Army was camped at the nearby village of Whitemarsh. When Morgan arrived at the American camp in November, he was ordered to watch for British movements along the Delaware River.

On December 7, Morgan's corps intercepted a British force that was marching to attack the American camp at Whitemarsh. The fighting was heavy—Morgan had a horse shot out from under him—but the Americans stopped the British. After this, Howe pulled his men back to Philadelphia for the winter. The Americans moved to Valley Forge, a hilly, wooded area about 20 miles west of the city. Morgan's men were ordered to patrol the approach to Valley Forge and warn Washington if they spotted British troops on the march.

AN IMPROVED CONTINENTAL ARMY

Morgan did not spend the entire winter at Valley Forge. Years of hard campaigning in bad weather had taken a toll on his health, so he was granted a *furlough* to visit his family.

American soldiers stand at attention as General Washington rides through the camp at Valley Forge. Although Morgan's men were assigned to guard a key route to the Continental camp, the ailing colonel was permitted to go home to Virginia for the winter.

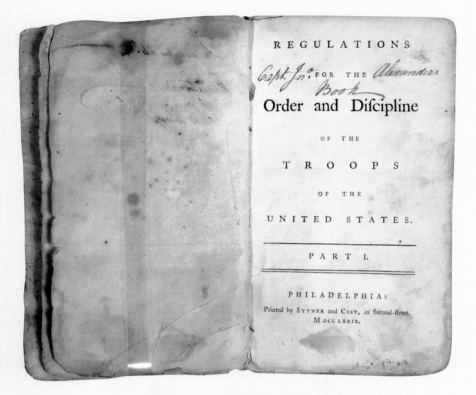

REGULATIONS

Capt. Jn.º FOR THE *Alexander Book*

Order and Difcipline

OF THE

T R O O P S

OF THE

U N I T E D   S T A T E S.

P A R T   I.

PHILADELPHIA:

Printed by STYNER and CIST, in Second-ftreet.
M DCC LXXIX.

The title page of Baron Friedrich Wilhelm von Steuben's manual, which he wrote to train the Continental Army. During the winter at Valley Forge, von Steuben took the raw American troops and turned them into a professional army.

He returned in May 1778 to find the Continental Army ready for a new campaign. A German officer named Baron von Steuben had helped train the Americans, turning them into a disciplined fighting force.

But British leaders were more concerned about the French than the Continental Army. They worried that the French navy would block the Delaware River and trap the British force in Philadelphia. After Howe resigned as commander and returned to England, Henry Clinton took over. General Clinton decided to bring all the British soldiers back to New York, and by June 1778 the redcoats were on the move.

Morgan's men were the first to enter Philadelphia when the British evacuated the capital, and they continued to follow as the redcoats marched into New Jersey. Washington assigned a militia unit to help Morgan's regiment, increasing his strength to about 600 men. The commander in chief also ordered Morgan to "take the most effectual means for gaining the enemy's right flank, and giving them as much annoyance as possible in that quarter." Once again, Morgan proved that his men were skilled at harassing the British. The Americans tore up bridges and cut down trees to slow the enemy's march. In one raid, they surprised and captured 15 British soldiers.

INCONCLUSIVE CLASH AT MONMOUTH

The British and American armies ultimately clashed at Monmouth Court House on June 28. Washington's second-in-command, General Charles Lee, was in charge of the initial attack. Early that morning Lee had told Morgan that he was going to attack. However, Lee did not explain where Morgan's corps needed to be or what the colonel was expected to do. Morgan waited for orders until 10 A.M. When he heard the sound of firing, Morgan sent messengers to find out what was going on.

The scene on the battlefield was chaotic. Lee's attack had been halfhearted and poorly planned, and when the British counterattacked he had retreated. Washington angrily relieved Lee of command and ordered the American soldiers to stand and fight. Morgan's regiment was too far away to play an effective role, so Washington told Morgan to stay where he was.

The Battle of Monmouth proved the value of von Steuben's training. After re-forming under Washington, the Americans held off repeated attacks by Clinton's best troops. The British suffered slightly higher casualties and withdrew from the field, allowing the Americans to claim victory.

Morgan was frustrated and disappointed to have missed the fighting. "If I had got notice of their situation . . . we could have taken most of [the retreating British], I think," he wrote to Washington. "We are all very unhappy that we did not share in the glory."

After the battle, Morgan's riflemen continued to harass the British as they marched to New York. But these were only skirmishes—no more large-scale battles were fought that year. In fact, Monmouth would be the last major battle fought in the North during the Revolution.

PASSED OVER FOR PROMOTION

In the fall of 1778, Morgan's rifle corps was dissolved, and he was given command of a regular Continental infantry

Washington rallies the American army at the Battle of Monmouth Court House. Because of a lack of direction by General Charles Lee, Morgan's men were out of position and could not take part in the battle. Lee was later court-martialed for his actions at Monmouth.

regiment. A short time later, he was temporarily appointed to command an entire brigade of Virginia troops. This was unusual, as brigadier generals, not colonels, normally led such large units. But General William Woodford, the brigade's commander, was sick, and Morgan was placed in charge until he recovered. The job involved more reports and paperwork than Morgan liked. However, he enjoyed the responsibility and soon became comfortable with the job. Morgan performed his duties well until Woodford returned in June 1779.

A week after turning the unit over to General Woodford, Morgan learned that a new brigade of light infantry was being formed. Morgan believed he deserved to be placed in command. He had a battlefield record that few

Continental officers could match. Plus, he had spent near-ly a year managing Woodford's brigade. However, the strange system by which officers were promoted in the Continental Army made it unlikely that he would get the position. Each colony was allotted a certain number of Continental officers, and Virginia already had more than its share of brigadier generals. In the end, Congress gave the light infantry brigade to General Anthony Wayne of Pennsylvania.

LEAVING THE ARMY

Morgan was extremely disappointed. He felt that by passing him over, Congress was showing that it did not respect his accomplishments. On June 30, 1779, he resigned from the army. George Washington was sorry to see Morgan leave, but he understood why the colonel was upset. Many other ambitious officers had been frustrated when they were not given promotions they felt they deserved. Wayne himself had threatened to leave the army if he did not receive command of the light infantry brigade. In a letter to Congress, Washington described Morgan as "a very valuable officer, who has rendered a series of important services, and distinguished himself on several occasions."

Morgan's wounded pride was not the only reason he wanted to leave the service. The 44-year-old colonel's health had not been good for several years. He had developed

Morgan was extremely disappointed when he was passed over for command of a newly formed brigade of light infantry in June 1779. Brigadier General Anthony Wayne (pictured), who received the command instead, won an important victory at Stony Point a few weeks later. By this time, however, Morgan had resigned from the army in disgust and returned to Winchester.

rheumatism, painful aches in his muscles and bones, after the frigid march to Canada. Another problem was *sciatica*, which caused sharp pains in his back and legs. These conditions were made worse by the uncomfortable and difficult living conditions of an army on the move.

Congress did not accept Morgan's resignation. Instead, Morgan was asked to consider himself on leave until a better position became available. He agreed, returning to his farm in Winchester. In his absence, it had been difficult for Abigail to keep up with the work. Taking care of the farm and enjoying time with his family kept Morgan busy during the fall of 1779. By winter, however, his sciatica had become so painful he could barely leave his bed.

THE WAR SHIFTS TO THE SOUTH

Morgan had chosen to leave the army at a time when there was little action. The British and Americans were at a deadlock in the northern colonies. But the British were developing a new strategy. General Clinton had decided to shift the war to the South, where there were greater numbers of Loyalists. Clinton thought that if British troops invaded the South, Loyalists in Georgia, South Carolina, and North Carolina would rise up against the Patriots. Once the southern colonies were back under British control, Clinton could move north and snuff out the rebellion.

By early 1780, while Morgan was still recovering from his sciatica, the British army had regained control of Georgia. Clinton next led an army to South Carolina, and on May 12, 1780, his men captured Charleston, the most important port in the South. When Charleston fell, 5,500 American soldiers were taken prisoner—the worst Patriot defeat of the war. Without the Continental Army to oppose them, the British were

Charles Cornwallis assumed command of the British army in South Carolina in June 1780. Within a few months, the aggressive general had nearly destroyed the Continental Army in the South and was preparing to invade North Carolina.

able to establish a string of small forts throughout South Carolina, from which they intended to impose royal rule on the colony. Events appeared to be going so well for the British that Clinton returned to New York in June, leaving his second-in-command, Lord Cornwallis, in charge.

A CIVIL WAR BEGINS

Soon, however, a brutal civil war broke out in South Carolina. During the early years of the war, when the Patriots were in power, they had repressed and bullied their Loyalist neighbors. When the British army arrived in 1780, Loyalists saw a chance to get even. Working with the British, armed Loyalists fought the rebels, arresting Patriot sympathizers and burning their homes. British commanders encouraged these tactics, believing that harsh treatment would stop others from opposing the king.

The *atrocities* angered many Americans who might otherwise have stayed out of the conflict, and they began fighting back. However, without an American army to keep the main British force occupied, it was only a matter of time before the British hunted down these rebels. In June 1780, Congress sent Horatio Gates to take charge of a new American army in the South.

The hero of Saratoga seemed to be a good choice for the job. In New York, Gates had proven that he could train and equip an army capable of defeating the British. Now he was being asked to do the same thing in the South. But Gates faced a difficult challenge. His new army consisted of fewer than 2,000 trained Continental soldiers and had little food, gunpowder, or other essential supplies.

DISASTER AT CAMDEN

Immediately after receiving his orders from Congress, Gates wrote to Morgan and asked him to take command of a special light infantry unit that he intended to create in the American southern army. Though interested, Morgan was still too sick to travel or fight. He told Gates that he would not rejoin the Continental Army until he was healthy.

Morgan was still recovering at home in August 1780 when he heard the news that the Continental Army had suffered another terrible defeat. Instead of strengthening his army, Gates had decided to attack the British garrison at Camden, South Carolina. Militia from North Carolina and Virginia had reinforced Gates, so the Americans slightly outnumbered the British. However, Cornwallis's men were better trained and better equipped. When the two armies clashed on August 16, 1780, the American militia broke and ran, and the British were able to destroy Gates's army. Two-thirds of the American soldiers were killed, wounded, or taken prisoner, and the British captured nearly all of the American army's artillery, muskets, and supplies.

6

TURNING POINT IN THE SOUTH

When Daniel Morgan heard about the disaster at Camden, he set out immediately for Hillsborough, North Carolina, where Gates had retreated with the remains of his army. Because of Morgan's bad back, the journey was slow and painful. He arrived in September 1780 to find just 700 poorly equipped soldiers. Morgan was placed in charge of a few hundred men and sent to help the North Carolina militia stop a British invasion of the state.

But the British were turned back before Morgan and his men arrived. On October 7, a band of backcountry Patriots destroyed a large Loyalist militia led by Major Patrick Ferguson at the Battle of King's Mountain. Cornwallis had planned to use Ferguson's militia to protect his supply lines while he invaded North Carolina. Without it, he had to return to South Carolina.

NEW COMMANDER IN THE SOUTH

On October 14, Major General Nathanael Greene was chosen to replace Gates as commander in the South. Although Greene had compiled an excellent war record while serving under George Washington in the northern campaigns, his task in the South seemed impossible. His army consisted of fewer than 1,000 trained soldiers. Georgia and South Carolina were firmly in British hands, and Virginia was struggling to repel a British army that had captured Richmond, cutting off a crucial supply line. But Greene had thought a lot about the situation and had developed a strategy for victory. He decided to break up his small army into three parts. He sent about 280 men, commanded by Lieutenant Colonel Henry "Light Horse Harry" Lee of Virginia, to help Francis Marion conduct his guerrilla war in the eastern part of South Carolina. Morgan was sent with about 600 men into western South Carolina to threaten the British outpost at Ninety-Six. Greene would move the rest of the army to Cheraw Hill, along the Pee Dee River in northeastern South Carolina.

Nathanael Greene was Washington's choice to take command in the South after the disastrous Battle of Camden. He found the American army weak and desperately in need of supplies. "Nothing can be more wretched and distressing than the condition of the troops, starving with cold and hunger, without tents and camp equipage," he wrote to Washington.

Greene knew dividing his army was dangerous, because Cornwallis's troops might destroy each of the units separately. But the British would have to catch the Americans first, and this was part of Greene's plan. If Cornwallis moved against Greene's army in northeastern South Carolina, Morgan and his men could capture Ninety-Six. This would break the British hold over the western part of South Carolina and encourage Patriots elsewhere in the state to resist. If the British general went after Morgan in the west, Greene could move south to join Marion and Lee in an attack on Charleston.

"THE FLYING ARMY"

Morgan received his orders on December 16. "You will employ [your soldiers] against the enemy on the west side of the [Catawba] river, either offensively or defensively, as your own prudence and discretion may direct," wrote Greene. "The object of this detachment is to give protection to that part of the country and spirit up the people, to annoy the enemy in that quarter."

Within a week Morgan's "flying army"—consisting of about 500 light infantry and 80 cavalry—had marched into South Carolina. On Christmas about 60 militiamen joined the Continentals. Their leader was General Andrew Pickens, a quiet, serious officer who was widely respected. Over the next few weeks, more militiamen from North Carolina and Georgia joined Morgan's Continentals, increasing his strength to nearly 1,000 men.

Morgan's first target was a Loyalist militia that was burning the homes of Patriots along Fair Forest Creek. He sent 80 cavalry and 200 mounted infantry after the Loyalists. Led by Morgan's cavalry commander, Lieutenant Colonel William Washington, the Continentals caught the Loyalists at a settlement known as Hammond's Store on December 30. Washington's men crushed the enemy, killing or wounding 150 Loyalists and capturing 40 without losing a man.

Lieutenant Colonel William Washington led Morgan's cavalry during his campaign in South Carolina. Washington, a second cousin of the American commander, was brave and determined in battle. "Washington is a Great Officer," Morgan later wrote.

This success encouraged Washington to attack a nearby British outpost, Fort William. By the time the Americans arrived, the worried British commander had abandoned the fort. Washington's men burned Fort William, then rejoined the main body of Morgan's force.

CORNWALLIS DISPATCHES TARLETON

The raids forced Cornwallis to react. As long as Morgan's army roamed freely in South Carolina, Loyalists would be afraid to help the British. Also, Cornwallis was afraid Morgan might capture Ninety-Six. In response, he divided his own force, sending some of his best soldiers after Morgan's men. On January 2, 1781, he wrote to his trusted commander Banastre Tarleton, "If Morgan is still at William's, or any where within your reach, I should wish you to push him to the utmost. Ninety-six is of so much consequence, that no time is to be lost."

Tarleton set out with about 800 men. He soon determined that Morgan was too far away to threaten Ninety-Six. On January 11, reinforcements increased Tarleton's numbers to about 1,200 men, and they moved to destroy Morgan's flying army. "Col. Tarleton is said to be on his way to pay you a visit," an anxious General Greene warned Morgan in a letter on January 13. "I doubt not but he will have a decent reception and a proper dismission."

By the time this message reached Morgan, he had already begun retreating north. This gave him a strategic advantage. If Tarleton followed, he would be moving farther away from Cornwallis's main army. The British would also have trouble finding food, as the Americans intended to seize all available supplies during their retreat.

"I WILL DEFEAT THE BRITISH OR LAY MY BONES"

The Americans barely managed to stay ahead of their pursuers. Early on the morning of January 16, Tarleton's men crossed the Pacolet River and marched toward the American position. When Morgan learned that the British were just a few miles away, he ordered the men to abandon their camp. Leaving their breakfasts burning over their campfires, the Patriots marched away as quickly as possible through swamps and rough terrain.

Following a hard march, Morgan's men arrived at the grassy open area known as Cowpens. His subordinates later recalled that after looking over the area, Morgan declared, "On this ground I will defeat the British or lay my bones."

Cowpens did not seem like an ideal battlefield for the Americans. There were no swamps or woods to hinder Tarleton's troops, and the flooded Broad River cut off the Patriots' escape. But Morgan knew that the only way he

Lieutenant Colonel John Eager Howard commanded a Continental regiment from Maryland. During the Revolution he fought bravely in many battles, including Germantown, Monmouth, and Camden. General Nathanael Greene wrote that Howard was "as good an officer as the world affords. He has great ability."

could be sure his militia would stand
and fight the British was to put them into an apparent trap. "I would not have had a swamp in view of my militia on any consideration; they would have made for it, and nothing could have detained them from it," he later wrote. "As to retreat, it was the very thing I wished to cut off all hope of. . . . When men are forced to fight, they will sell their lives dearly."

Understanding the limitations of his militia, Morgan developed an unusual battle plan. The Americans would form three lines, each separated by about 150 yards. In the front row, armed with rifles, would be experienced militiamen from Georgia, North Carolina, and Virginia. These men were excellent shots and would be able to pick off British soldiers when they arrived on the battlefield. But they could not withstand a bayonet charge. Morgan's plan called for the riflemen to fire three times as the British approached, then run back to the second line. This row, containing the rest of the militia and commanded by Andrew Pickens, would fire two volleys as the British approached. The militia would then retreat behind the third line, composed of trained Continental troops led by Lieutenant Colonel John Eager Howard. After re-forming, the militia could be sent back into the battle. Washington's cavalry would be held back, to be used wherever needed.

THE BATTLE OF COWPENS

Morgan spent the night explaining his plan to the men. When morning came, there was just enough time for the American soldiers to eat a quick breakfast before they had to form their battle lines in the dewy grass. When the redcoats charged toward the American lines, screaming their battle cry, Morgan roared encouragement to his men. "They give us the British halloo, boys," he shouted. "Give them the Indian whoop."

After each of the riflemen in the first line had fired several shots, they drifted back into Pickens's line as planned. Major Young later recalled that Morgan "galloped along the lines, cheering the men, and telling them not to fire until we could see the whites of their eyes." Once the British were within 50 yards, the American militiamen in the second line fired two devastating volleys. Huge gaps appeared in the British lines as wounded men fell to the ground, but the redcoats continued their bayonet charge.

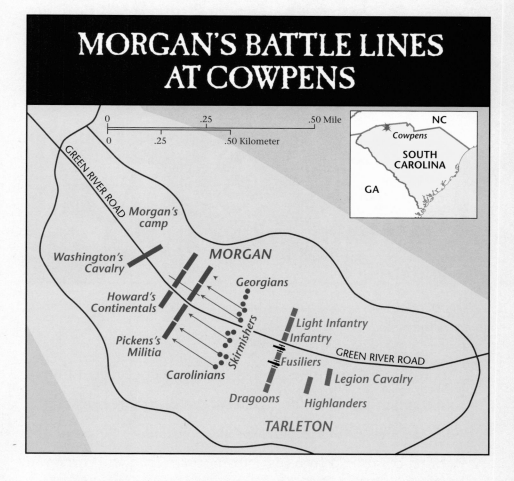

MORGAN'S BATTLE LINES AT COWPENS

So far, Morgan's plan had worked, but now a problem developed. As the second line of militia began to withdraw, some of the men panicked. Tarleton saw the Americans' orderly retreat start to become chaotic, and he sent in his cavalry to cut the enemy down. But just as the British horsemen reached the militia, Washington's men pounded in from the side. The surprise attack sent the British cavalry reeling with heavy losses.

At the same time, Morgan and his officers were desperately trying to turn the militia back toward the battlefield.

William Washington's cavalry surprises Tarleton's dragoons as they are preparing to attack the militia.

"Form, form, my brave fellows!" Morgan cried, according to militiaman James Collins. "Give them one more fire and the day is ours. Old Morgan was never beaten!" Some of the militia continued running, but most stopped and turned to face the enemy again.

Meanwhile, the Continentals and redcoats were engaged in fierce combat. "The fire on both sides was well supported, and produced much slaughter," Tarleton later wrote. In some places, the Americans and British engaged in deadly hand-to-hand combat. On the right side of the American line, a British charge forced the Continentals to pull back. But the retreating Americans turned suddenly and fired a devastating volley at close range. "[The] unexpected fire . . . stopped the British and threw them into confusion," observed Tarleton.

"The ground was instantly covered with the bodies of the killed and wounded, and a total rout ensued."

At that moment, Pickens's re-formed militia reentered the battle, while Washington's cavalry charged into the British ranks. The exhausted British could take no more. Many dropped their weapons and surrendered, while others ran away. Tarleton, leading the British cavalry, bravely tried to rally his men. But he soon realized the battle was lost and raced from the field, followed by about 60 horsemen.

SIGNIFICANCE OF THE VICTORY

The Battle of Cowpens was among the greatest American victories of the Revolution. Morgan's men captured more than 700 British soldiers and killed 110; on the American side, 12 men were killed and 60 wounded. Cowpens encouraged Patriots in the South to keep fighting, and it weakened the British army considerably. Cornwallis needed Tarleton's fast-moving British Legion to scout for the enemy and strike fear into the Patriots. Without the Legion, the British general was at a significant disadvantage.

Most important, Cornwallis's reaction to Cowpens started a series of events that would result in an American triumph. The British general was so angry when he learned about Tarleton's defeat that he set out with his entire army to catch Morgan. First, though, he ordered his supply wagons to be burned so that his men could travel faster. This rash decision

Continental soldiers overwhelm the British 7th Regiment of Foot during the final stages of the Battle of Cowpens.

would haunt Cornwallis over the next nine months. As the British chased the Continentals through North Carolina and into Virginia, they had trouble finding food and supplies. With his army weakened and starving, and facing a tough challenge from the revitalized Continental Army, Cornwallis headed for the Virginia coast. He hoped for rescue by the British navy, but the fleet never arrived. On October 19, 1781, Cornwallis was forced to surrender his army at York-town.

7

FINAL YEARS

Daniel Morgan was not with the Continental Army at Yorktown. Cowpens would be the general's last major battle of the Revolution. Soon after rejoining Greene in North Carolina in late January, Morgan suffered another flare-up of his health problems. On February 10, 1781, he was allowed to return home to rest.

By May 1781, Morgan was feeling good enough to raise a company of Virginia riflemen to help the Marquis de Lafayette during his campaign in Virginia. But after leading the new soldiers to Lafayette's camp at Malvern Hill, Morgan became sick once again, and he returned home in early August. This time, the illness was more serious. Morgan later wrote to a friend that he had been near death for weeks.

The general was feeling much better when he heard about the British surrender at Yorktown. Perhaps a letter from George Washington lifted his spirits. Writing on October 5, 1781, during the siege of Yorktown, Washington praised Morgan's military service. "Be assured that I most sincerely lament your present Situation, and esteem it a peculiar Loss to the United States, that you are, at this Time, unable to render your services in the Field," Washington wrote.

The British surrender at Yorktown essentially marked the end of the American Revolution. The British people were not interested in continuing King George's costly war.

Once the British surrendered at Yorktown in October 1781, the American Revolution was all but over. Although Morgan's bad health kept him from taking part in the siege of Yorktown, Washington and other Patriot leaders acknowledged that his efforts in South Carolina had helped make the American victory possible.

Though sporadic fighting still occurred, in 1783 British and American representatives signed a treaty in Paris that officially ended the war. America had won its independence.

PRIVATE CITIZEN

As Morgan recovered his health, he stayed busy with private pursuits. In 1782 Morgan oversaw construction of a large stone house, which he called Saratoga, on his farm near Winchester. He purchased other large tracts of land as well, and started several businesses in partnership with a friend named Nathaniel Burwell.

Morgan's army friends occasionally visited him at Saratoga, and he wrote them regular letters. But he particularly liked spending time with his wife and family. Both of Morgan's daughters married former officers in the Continental Army. Nancy Morgan married Presley Neville and moved to Pittsburgh, where they had 15 children. Betsy Morgan married James Heard and remained in the Winchester area. They had four children. When Morgan's grandchildren visited Saratoga, he enjoyed telling them stories about his military adventures.

THE WHISKEY REBELLION

In 1794 Morgan put on his uniform once again. This time, he was called upon to help put down an uprising in western Pennsylvania called the Whiskey Rebellion. Farmers upset about a tax on whiskey had revolted during the summer of 1794. Angry mobs assaulted tax collectors, robbed mail coaches, interfered with court proceedings, and threatened to attack Pittsburgh.

To end the Whiskey Rebellion, President George Washington called out more than 12,000 militiamen from nearby states. Morgan was chosen to train and lead Virginia's militia. In October, Washington led the militia into western

In this letter to President Washington, written in April 1795, Morgan discusses the situation in western Pennsylvania. "It shall be my Endeavour to settle all Disputes as amicably as possible," the general promised.

Pennsylvania, and the grumbling farmers surrendered. By late November the president had returned to the capital, leaving Morgan to keep the peace in the region with a few thousand soldiers.

Morgan quickly took steps to bring all sides together. He told his men not to harass the former rebels, and he sought pardons for some of the leaders. His actions helped ease tensions. Washington praised his work in a letter written on March 27, 1795: "It has afforded me great pleasure to learn, that the general conduct and character of the Army has been temperate and indulgent, and that your attention to the quiet and comfort of the western inhabitants has been well received by them."

The Whiskey Rebellion was an important test of the new federal government. Washington's prompt response showed citizens that the federal government would use force to end threats to the peace. If people wanted to change the law, they would have to do so peacefully.

POLITICAL CAREER

Even before the Whiskey Rebellion had ended, Morgan decided that he wanted to help make the new country's laws. Morgan admired George Washington and supported "Federalist" policies formulated by Washington's secretary of the Treasury, Alexander Hamilton. He disliked the new Republican Party, formed by Thomas Jefferson and James

Madison to oppose the Federalists. In the 1795 election to Congress, Morgan decided to run against a Republican named Robert Rutherford, who had been involved in Virginia's government for many years. However, Morgan was too busy in western Pennsylvania to spend much time campaigning, and he lost the election.

In the next election two years later, Morgan again challenged Rutherford. This time, he won a seat in the U.S. House of Representatives. In May 1797, Morgan traveled to the capital, Philadelphia, to take his place in Congress. As a congressman, he voted to increase the size of the navy and supported the Sedition Act, a controversial law that made it a crime for people to criticize the government and its policies. But he did not make a major impact as a legislator. Because his health was poor, Morgan decided not to run for a second term.

SOLDIER'S REST

After returning to Virginia in February 1799, Morgan sold Saratoga and moved back to a smaller house he owned, called Soldier's Rest. In 1800 he moved into a house in Winchester, where he could get regular medical care. In his last days, Morgan grew very interested in religion. He became friendly with the pastor of Winchester's Presbyterian church, attending church services when he was able. But during the final year of his life, Morgan was so weak that he could barely leave his house.

On July 6, 1802, General Daniel Morgan died at age 67. He was buried in Winchester and mourned throughout the nation. At his funeral, seven members of his former rifle company fired their weapons over his grave in a final military salute for the Old Wagoner.

For many years, Americans recognized the name and remembered the accomplishments of Daniel Morgan. In 1820, when Virginia created a new county in the northern part of the state, it was named for Morgan. (Today, Morgan County is part of West Virginia.) Alabama, Georgia, Illinois, Indiana, Kentucky, Missouri, Ohio, and Tennessee also named counties in Morgan's honor. But over the decades, Morgan's contributions to the American Revolution faded from popular memory as attention came to focus on men such as Washington, Benjamin Franklin, Thomas Jefferson, and John Adams. This is unfortunate, for without Daniel Morgan the Revolution might have been lost.

Morgan was arguably the greatest battlefield tactician of the Revolutionary War, as demonstrated by his remarkable successes at Saratoga and Cowpens, as well as in numerous minor battles and skirmishes. His bravery and leadership made American independence possible. Daniel Morgan deserves to be remembered as one of America's foremost military leaders of the Revolution.

Chronology

1735 or 1736: Daniel Morgan is born, probably in Hunterdon County, New Jersey, during wintertime.

1753: Arrives in the Winchester, Virginia, area and takes work with a local farmer.

1755: While working as a freight hauler, accompanies General Braddock's British army on the ill-fated march to Fort Duquesne; after returning to Winchester, joins a company of rangers and is sent to defend the Virginia frontier.

1756: In April, is ambushed by Indians and wounded near Fort Edwards.

1758: Resumes career as an independent freight hauler.

1761: Begins courting Abigail Curry, the daughter of a Winchester-area farmer; serves as a lieutenant in a militia company during Chief Pontiac's War, but does not see action.

1771: Purchases a 255-acre farm near Winchester.

1773: Marries Abigail Curry, who has already given birth to his two daughters, Nancy and Betsy.

1774: Fights Indians as a militia captain during Lord Dunmore's War.

1775: On April 19, the battles of Lexington and Concord begin the American Revolution; Morgan is chosen to lead a company of frontier riflemen from Frederick County; joins the Continental Army in Boston; selected to take part in the invasion of Canada; after a grueling march, Morgan leads his soldiers into Quebec but is captured.

1776: Morgan spends most of the year as a British prisoner; in July, the United States of America declares independence from Great Britain; in September, Morgan is permitted to return home to Winchester on parole.

1777: After a prisoner exchange, Morgan is permitted to rejoin the Continental Army and is promoted to colonel; harasses General Howe's British troops in New Jersey during June and July; in August, sent to western New York to help stop the British army commanded by General John Burgoyne; plays a key role in the battles of Freeman's

Farm and Bemis Heights, which lead to Burgoyne's surrender at Saratoga on October 17.

1778: Conducts an active campaign against the British in New Jersey; in the fall, placed in temporary command of General William Woodford's brigade.

1779: After Woodford returns to duty, Morgan asks for command of a new light infantry brigade; when his request is rejected, he decides to resign from the army; returns to his farm at Winchester, but is soon disabled by illness.

1780: British troops capture Charleston in May; on August 16, Gates is defeated at Camden; on October 7, the Overmountain Men defeat Major Patrick Ferguson's militia at the Battle of King's Mountain; in December, Nathanael Greene takes command of the Continental Army in the South and sends Morgan to threaten Ninety-Six.

1781: On January 17, Morgan's "flying army" engages a 1,200-man force commanded by Banastre Tarleton, winning a decisive victory at Cowpens; Morgan is forced to leave the army and return home because of illness; on October 19, General Cornwallis surrenders his army at Yorktown.

1782: Work is completed on Morgan's home, Saratoga.

1783: The Treaty of Paris is signed in September, officially ending the American Revolution.

1794: Morgan is placed in charge of Virginia's militia, called out to put down a revolt in western Pennsylvania known as the Whiskey Rebellion; once the rebels surrender, Morgan is placed in charge of the militia force that occupies the region to keep peace.

1795: Morgan runs unsuccessfully for Congress.

1797: Morgan defeats incumbent Robert Rutherford to win a term in Congress.

1799: In February, illness forces Morgan to leave Congress before it adjourns; he is unable to run for a second term.

1802: Dies on July 6 and is buried in the cemetery of the Winchester Presbyterian church.

Glossary

atrocity—a shockingly cruel act of violence against an enemy during wartime.

brigade—a military unit consisting of two or more regiments; during the American Revolution, a typical Continental brigade numbered about 1,600 to 2,400 men.

forage—to search for food or supplies.

foray—a sudden attack or raid by a military force.

furlough—a leave of absence from military duty.

Loyalist—a person who remained loyal to King George III and the British government during the American Revolution.

mercenary—a professional soldier who is paid to fight for an army other than that of his country.

militia—an army of civilian volunteers called out to serve in emergencies. Militias often had limited training, and soldiers often had to provide their own muskets.

outflank—to go around the main body of an enemy force and attack it from the side or behind.

parole—the release of a prisoner of war who has pledged to honor certain conditions (for example, not to resume fighting for a specified period).

Patriot—a colonist who opposed Parliament and King George III before and during the American Revolution.

portage—to carry or transport boats or cargo across land from one waterway to another.

redoubt—a temporary defensive fortification.

rheumatism—a painful condition of the joints or muscles.

sciatica—pain and tenderness in the lower back and legs.

siege—a military operation in which an army surrounds an enemy fortification and cuts off outside access in an effort to force a surrender.

skirmish—a brief fight involving small units of larger armies.

stalemate—a situation in which both sides are evenly matched, and neither can clearly win.

stockade—a simple, crude fort built with wooden posts and used to defend the frontier.

tactics—the science of organizing and maneuvering forces in battle to achieve victory.

teamster—somebody who drives a team of animals used for hauling.

Further Reading

Books for Students:

Aronson, Marc. *The Real Revolution: The Global Story of American Independence*. New York: Clarion Books, 2005.

Fleming, Thomas. *Liberty! The Story of the American Revolution*. New York: Viking, 1997.

Schanzer, Rosalyn. *George vs. George: The American Revolution as Seen from Both Sides*. Hanover, Pa.: National Geographic Books, 2004.

Sheinkin, Steve. *The American Revolution*. Stamford, Conn.: Summer Street Press, 2005.

Strum, Richard. *Causes of the American Revolution*. Stockton, N.J.: OTTN Publishing, 2005.

Books for Older Readers:

Babits, Lawrence E. *A Devil of a Whipping: The Battle of Cowpens*. Chapel Hill: University of North Carolina Press, 1998.

Buchanan, John. *The Road to Guilford Courthouse: The American Revolution in the Carolinas*. New York: John Wiley and Sons, 1997.

Edgar, Walter. *Partisans and Redcoats: The Southern Conflict that Turned the Tide of the American Revolution*. New York: Perennial, 2001.

Graham, James. *The Life of General Daniel Morgan*. New York: Derby and Jackson, 1856. (Reprint edition: University of Michigan Library, 2001.)

Higginbotham, Don. *Daniel Morgan: Revolutionary Rifleman*. Chapel Hill: University of North Carolina Press, 1961.

LaCrosse, Richard B. *Revolutionary Rangers: Daniel Morgan's Riflemen and their Role on the Northern Frontier, 1778–1783*. Bowie, Md.: Heritage Books, 2002.

Middlekauff, Robert. *The Glorious Cause: The American Revolution, 1763–1789*. 2nd edition. New York: Oxford University Press, 2005.

Wood, W. J. *Battles of the Revolutionary War, 1775–1781*. Cambridge, Mass.: Da Capo Press, 2003.

http://www.nps.gov/cowp/dmorgan.htm

A biographical article about Daniel Morgan prepared by a National Park Service ranger at Cowpens National Battlefield.

http://memory.loc.gov/ammem/gwhtml/

The Library of Congress has made more than 150,000 pages of George Washington's correspondence, including many letters to or about Daniel Morgan, available online. The George Washington Papers can be searched, and transcripts are available of many letters.

http://www.nps.gov/sara/s-batles.htm

This page, maintained by the National Park Service at Saratoga National Historical Park, contains an explanation of the Saratoga campaign as well as information about key figures and events.

http://www.americaslibrary.gov/cgi-bin/page.cgi/jb/revolut

This Library of Congress website provides information about people and events of the American Revolution.

http://www.thewarthatmadeamerica.org/

The companion website to the 2006 PBS documentary *The War that Made America* provides interesting facts about the French and Indian War, as well as biographies of key figures.

http://www.fortedwards.org/colonial/morgan.htm

This website includes pictures and information about Daniel Morgan's homes in the Winchester area. It is operated by the Fort Edwards Foundation, which maintains the British post where Morgan served during the French and Indian War.

http://www.usahistory.info/south/war.html

This website provides information about the American Revolution in the South.

Index

Numbers in **bold italics** refer to captions.

Picture Credits

About the Author

JIM GALLAGHER is the author of more than 20 books for young readers, including *Causes of the Iraq War, The Johnstown Flood*, and *Ferdinand Magellan and the First Voyage Around the World*. He lives in New Jersey with his wife, LaNelle, and their sons, Donald and Dillon.